MW01641162

INTERNATIONAL
BOW
TIE
SOCIETY

"Bow ties are not just a fashion option. A bow tie is a lifestyle statement of discerning individualists comfortable in their own skin."

-International Bow Tie Society (IBTS)

In memory of the ***Patron Saint*** *of bow ties:*

Sir Winston Churchill

"If you have an important point to make, don't try to be subtle or clever. Use a pile driver. Hit the point once. Then come back and hit it again. Then hit it a third time—a tremendous whack."

— Winston Churchill

Dedicated to two enthusiastic young men who have never worn any neckwear except free-style bow ties. They both went from diapers to dapper... from bibs to bow ties!

Jack Ketchel – 7 years old
Chase Ketchel – 6 years old
Lifetime members in good standing of the...
International Bow Tie Society

Illustrations and logos drawn very professionally by Rob McElhaney and Caitlin Rantala
Extraordinary talents!

Contact through www.internationalbowtiesociety.com

The first ever…

BOW TIE BIBLE

Seriously funny guide to how and why to bow tie

History-Etiquette-Resurgence

Chuck Blackburn—Founder

International Bow Tie Society

chuck@internationalbowtiesociety.com
www.InternationalBowTieSociety.com
Facebook.com/internationalbowtiesociety

INTERNATIONAL
BOW
TIE
SOCIETY

Contents

INTERNATIONAL
BOW
TIE
SOCIETY

Preface

***Impossible to know what you don't know*–** Whether you're into bow ties or not, we invite you to have a little fun allowing yourself to learn some possibly surprising facts guaranteed to make you scratch your head and smile!

***Some were called*—**The original authors of the *real* thousand-plus-page Bible—not to be confused with this absurdly satirical Bow Tie Bible—were "called" to write God's message to humanity on parchment scrolls chronicling the beginning of time.

We at the International Bow Tie Society (IBTS) believe we were called to pen this parodied Bow Tie Bible. We say this not to put ourselves on a par with the original Bible authors but to point out a need for everyone to understand the "how's and wherefores" of making a statement of style and individuality in a world unwittingly conformed to wearing long ties.

While the real Bible's authors had the assistance of God and the Holy Spirit in writing their books, we merely had the Internet, Google, and iPhone. We contacted bow tie manufacturers and retailers worldwide. We have talked with thousands of bow tie wearers as well as those who never thought twice about bow ties.

We spent thirty-five years shopping for and wearing hundreds of bow ties worldwide. We've manufactured, designed, and marketed neckwear to the finest men's specialty shops in the country.

Besides, a comprehensive exposé of the bow tie world was much overdue and, with no one else really interested in researching bow tie history and etiquette, if not by us...then by whom? We felt bow ties had been misunderstood and even maligned so we do this to set the record straight once and for all.

Bow ties are coming back and the IBTS feel duty-bound to tell men what they need to know, not only how to tie one, but what to know how and why to wear one!

It is not our intension to be "anti" long ties and hopefully we don't seem defensive. However, we don't mind showing our unwavering "anti-conformity" predisposition. We want the world to know there are logical, rational, and even laudable reasons many men have yet to consider regarding bow ties.

When learned, well-dressed men appreciate the pros and cons of bow ties compared with long ties, it will help them see bow-ties-done-right more receptively and hopefully, more positively. Then, like Paul on the road to Damascus, they will *see the light!*

We hope you enjoy the story. We wrote it for you!

"When I was four years old they tried to test my IQ, they showed me a picture of three oranges and a pear. They asked me which one is different and does not belong; they taught me different was wrong."

—Ani Difranco

I
II
III
VI
VII
VIII
IX
X

Ten Commandments of Bow Ties

I. Thou shalt never wear pre-tied or "clip-on" bow ties.
II. Thou shalt not wear bow ties horizontally wider or vertically taller than your eye sockets.
III. Thou shalt not wear bow ties so neat and symmetrical as to appear pre-tied.
IV. Thou shalt not wait past age 12 to learn how to properly tie a bow tie.
V. Thou shalt volunteer to help others learn to properly tie bow ties.
VI. Thou shalt assist others in understanding how and why one would choose to wear bow ties, especially if they are relatives.
VII. Thou shalt tactfully correct others wearing bow ties improperly.
VIII. Thou shalt learn how to communicate to others why you prefer bow ties as a positive alternative to long ties.
IX. Thou shalt own at *least* two dozen properly sized and shaped quality, handmade bow ties you love to wear.
X. Thou shalt suggest friends, family, and colleagues to go to International Bow Tie Society.com and join free or pay a little for more benefits today even if they are not into bow ties.

Chapter One

Genesis

In the beginning God created the heavens and the earth. Now, some disturbing revelations have come to light regarding God's creation of the first human on earth.

Caution: Proceed at your own peril. What you're about to learn could produce disturbing questions in your mind. But we invite you to suspend your most cherished core beliefs and allow a stretch of your imagination. And now that you've been duly warned don't blame us if this changes your reality forever!

We have no quarrel with God's omniscience and omnipotence. That notwithstanding, we find it difficult to dispute evidence that God may have allowed himself to fall prey to "old-fashioned" boredom and distraction regarding the manner in which he created Adam, the first man.

Naturally, every thinking person would readily see that in the beginning everything was unprecedented, deeming nothing to truly be old-fashioned! Nevertheless, taking large dollops of poetic license we conclude that the boredom and distraction notion is not only plausible, but also probable!

First, consider that God created everything from the stars to the planets to the animals—including the tiniest insects—prior to taking time to craft his very first human being, Adam.

Let's get this timeline straight...God took the first five days of his self-imposed, seven-day deadline to create the entire universe and all of nature (in perfect harmony) before deeming it an appropriate time to start, and complete, the important and difficult process of making mankind from scratch? No wonder he rested on the seventh day!

And we are quick to point out a few observations most may not have considered regarding God's leading man. Adam was *not* born so he didn't truly have a birthday—he was created as a fully grown human being. Adam had no parents, no childhood, no youth, no formative years, and later, if someone might—out of curiosity—ask where he grew up, Adam would be forced to honestly reply, "*Nowhere!*"

Adam had no siblings, no primary or secondary education, no experience to draw from or learn from, no apparent social skills, no friends, and no clothing! All things considered, isn't it plausible, entirely possible, that the process God used to create his very first man—spitting on the ground and molding a fully grown man out of a lump of clay—was more or less an afterthought?

Let's pause to allow us to officially take another stab at what will be a series of disclaimers to salvage our credibility. We wouldn't blame anyone for castigating us as blasphemous by suggesting, even in jest, God cut a few corners in his race to make a hard deadline...even if it was a deadline of his own making. After all, God may have been a little worn out after those first five days creating everything else before taking that very last work day to begin the daunting task of creating man. And being that tuckered out perhaps he was contemplating a restful Sunday afternoon nap. Who's to say? God only knows.

But, doesn't it beg the question...what was God's rush? Would it have hurt to take a few extra days to *perfect* mankind—since it is arguably his greatest creation of all eternity?

Rational people with the slightest familiarity of Bible history are forced to entertain the notion that Adam needed some additional *tweaking* before God rolled him off the assembly line.

Consider the problems man caused God right off the bat! Adam and Eve disobeyed God by eating the forbidden fruit; Cain killed his brother Abel for no good reason. Recall the Tower of Babel, and the Great Flood. Is it just us? Or would you, the reader, once again temporarily leave your long-held, sacred beliefs and arrive at some logical conclusions? Possibly a drink of Communion wine would help?

"Conformity crushes the spirit and smothers the soul."

—Anonymous

If the IBTS had created man...

Meanwhile, are you curious about how this relates to bow ties? All right, take the International Bow Tie Society's perspective. If IBTS had God's unlimited power and knowledge to create mankind from scratch, what kind of man would *we* create? Our man would *not* be indifferent, closed-minded, or resistant to at least considering bow ties in today's predominantly long tie world.

In retrospect, we would prefer God had created a discerning, self-confident nonconformist. We would be better served by a thoughtful man who could, after considering the plethora of facts regarding why certain well-dressed men could possess sufficient audacity and independence to make a personal statement sporting a properly tied bow tie in a roomful of men conforming to the norm...long ties!

That also being said, members of IBTS are forever thankful for God's consolation prize. Even though we feel God may have rushed his process in creating Adam, he did give him a neck! And since Adam was the prototype, necks became standard equipment for all of Adam's predecessors. And this seemingly trivial factoid is especially utilitarian because you, our very intelligent and enlightened reader, have just completed the first chapter of the first ever Bow Tie Bible.

"Custom will reconcile people into any atrocity; and fashion will drive them to acquire any custom."

- George Bernard Shaw

Chapter Two

Why a Bow Tie Bible?

The Bow Tie Bible attempts to expose, define, and showcase the bow tie culture about to experience a paradigm shift in our predominately long tie world. We pose questions like, "Why would a presumably well-educated, well-dressed stylish man—without engaging in any thought process—bind his neck with an often uncomfortable, somewhat impractical, usually more expensive, surprisingly unsanitary, long silk tie while ignoring what a bow tie can do as a personal statement of style and self-confidence as a discerning individualist?"

Do not let our ranting mislead you—bow ties are not for everyone. Not every man considers it important to be well dressed, and many disparage wearing any neckwear whatsoever. That's perfectly OK. And many, even though they may fit the criteria of a confident and discerning individualist—are not aware of, or motivated to consider, the pros and cons of making *any* statement with their choice of neckwear or any type of clothing.

Why don't more men wear bow ties? Part of the reason must be having really never seen or experienced great bow ties worn properly.

They may also be plagued by nightmares evoking painful memories about when they were forced to wear oversized, pre-tied, clip-on, ugly polyester bow ties as a kid. Or while on a date to the prom in a rented dinner jacket they looked at themselves in the mirror and felt ridiculous and self-conscious, as maybe they should. And much to their chagrin, their proud parents took loads of photos displaying their child's embarrassment to friends and family! All these negative stimuli can, over time, brainwash even the strongest willed among us.

Changing the bow tie stereotype

We at IBTS wonder if otherwise intelligent and worldly gentlemen might be harboring a variety of negative stereotypes buried deep in their subconscious, maybe dating back decades. These negative experiences, coupled with seeing others (even high-profile celebrities) improperly wearing bow ties, scares and thus deters these otherwise open-minded men from breaking away from deep-seeded adverse preconceptions.

From our group's observations, research, and collaboration, we have compiled what we believe to be the most common negative bow tie stereotypes:

- Only kids, comedians, clowns, eccentric professors (with pipes and comfortable shoes), or ice cream vendors wear bow ties.
- One cannot trust a man in a bow tie. (Really? If you have to wear a long tie to gain people's trust, you probably have bigger issues.)
- Bow tie wearers are show-offs needing extra attention or affection.
- Bow tie wearers are too weird. Why don't they just conform to long ties like the rest of us?
- Bow ties seem too dressy or too casual.
- Bow ties are suggestive of alternative lifestyles of which one chooses not to identify.
- Bow ties look goofy.

Like most negative stereotypes they make no sense. They are grounded on preconceived feelings rather than reality! They are hogwash.

However, some of these stereotypes have a great deal of validity because so many are focused so much on "how" to tie a bow tie they have little regard for knowing the size, shape, and styling that would be most flattering and professional for them.

Never wider nor taller than one's eye-sockets…

We might go a little further to say the majority of negative stereotypes are perpetrated by gentlemen wearing bow ties that, although properly tied and stylish, otherwise miss the mark. This is especially onerous when an unknowing gentleman wears an expensive bow tie that's too wide or too tall for his facial features or the shape of his head or neck.

In the fashion world there is a great deal of latitude regarding size; however, there are traditionally some accepted rules. Suit jackets, sport coats, trousers, and shirts should fit! Sure, we see trendy or ethnic anomalies like sleeves to the knuckles, "pants on the ground," or cut-up jeans; but—for true gentlemen—certain articles should properly fit to look proper and professional.

Bow ties are the closest article of clothing to one's face, so they look best when they **fit the face**. Wearing a bow tie an eighth-inch too narrow or an eighth-inch too short looks perfectly fine. However, that same well-dressed, intelligent individual wearing exactly the same bow tie even one eighth-inch too wide or an eighth-inch too tall looks silly...really goofy! Properly sized bow ties should never, *ever* be larger than one's eye sockets.

A little difference makes a big impression! One (upper left) says, “Look at me; I’m wearing a bow tie!”

The other (lower right) confidently communicates, “This is how to wear a bow tie.”

What the fashion industry isn't telling us...

The fashion industry is not helping us advance our cause. Fashionistas know it is not in their best interest financially gentlemen to suddenly embrace the bow tie culture and switch away from long ties. However, as fashions change; eye sockets do not.

We can only spread the word that bow ties are more comfortable, stylish, and practical while less expensive. They never get in the way and are far less likely to be ruined and replaced due to mealtime accidents or inadvertent sneezing mishaps.

It takes time to change generations of conformity, social conditioning, and fashion industry indoctrination. It's difficult to educate anyone unmotivated to learn and resistant to change. We, however, are up to the challenge. We are aware the longest journey begins with a single **Bow Tie Bible**.

One thing might accelerate the transition—if a gentleman experiences the feeling of adoration proffered by a comely, bright woman when genuinely complimenting him on the way he looks in a bow tie! Of course, this requires that this gentleman understands there is a right way and wrong way to do anything. This is especially so considering the afore-mentioned negative stereotypes.

"The reward for conformity is that everyone likes you but yourself."

—Rita Mae Brown

Again our challenge is to educate well-dressed men on how and why properly sized and tied bow ties need to be congruent with their facial features to look professional.

Men must experience positive feelings for themselves. They need to only stick their toe into the warm, inviting water before taking the plunge. Starting in the right direction has much to do with gradually developing self-confidence vital to sustainable success.

The challenge facing IBTS

We are not naïve regarding human behavior. Logical thinking rarely trumps emotions. After all, God created mankind with the free will to make misguided decisions based on misinformation sans rational thinking resulting in absolutely senseless behavior! Case in point, why would Adam and Eve immediately ignore God's only warnings and trade a perfect life on earth for one lousy bite of a really bad apple? And, for that matter, why do people fool themselves into thinking that drinking diet sodas will counteract their wolfing down hot apple pie á la mode after a thick prime rib dinner, with a loaded baked potato, lobster bisque, and a blue cheese drenched salad?

We also learned, vicariously, that answering the more essential questions of *how* and *why* one might consider bow ties-versus-long ties is more critical even than one being proficient in tying one. Again, anyone can learn to tie a bow tie if they really *want* to learn; but few know how and why to wear bow ties in the first place.

As stated, the Bow Tie Bible was written to advance that message.

When God created man and gave him a neck, he also equipped man with a mind. And that mind is something today's well-dressed man has total liberty to change anytime—at will—when considering new, irrefutable, common-sense information. We will imitate Solomon's wisdom in hopes that men will realize it is in their best interest not to split the baby!
(That last sentence may be confusing to anyone not familiar with King Solomon's most famous judgment.)

If you think it's easy to change someone else's mind...just see how hard it is to change your own!

Please excuse a personal note. My dear grandmother shared some wisdom with me long ago before I was old enough to understand. She told me:
"If you've decided you can *never* change your mind—why have one?"

Chapter Three

Learning Some of the Basics

But let's not get too sidetracked... Back to the story—it's riveting!

Those of you who have even a passing knowledge of the Bible will recall Adam was, of course, completely sans clothing—naked as a jaybird—while inhabiting the Garden of Eden. And before Eve took his spare rib Adam—bless his heart—couldn't have possibly known anything about fashion, neckwear, or in that case, women! How could he? There was absolutely no precedence, no experience, and no scrolls to draw from as to what God was up to next.

Fact is, even if Adam had clothing, his wardrobe would most probably have ***not*** included collared shirts. And, since there was only one woman—he couldn't have thought about impressing her. Nor did he have any idea how to gain the respect of his peers. You might say—tongue-in-cheek—Adam was peerless!

This is additional evidence of the "unintended consequences" controversy regarding Adam and Eve's fall from grace can be partially attributed to Adam's ignorance regarding the opposite sex!

"Follow the path of the unsafe, independent thinker. Expose your ideas to the danger of controversy. Speak your mind and fear less the label of **crackpot** ***than the stigma of conformity."***

—Thomas J. Watson

Because Adam and Eve sinned...we have bow ties! And as we have repeated vociferously, when well-meaning gentlemen wear bow ties a little too big, it hurts their image and deleteriously affects the bow tie world. Just a little *too big* challenges the professional, sophisticated image we all work toward.

Again, how big is too big? As mentioned and illustrated, no bigger than your eye sockets is the rule of thumb. You can usually reduce the horizontal width by reducing the entire length of the bow tie an inch or so smaller than your shirt neck measurement until it ties no wider than the inner edge of our eye sockets or the width of your neck—whichever is narrower. We don't need to look like Bozo, or a kid in an oversized clip-on tie going to the Easter egg hunt.

The horizontal width is easier to adjust if the shape of the tie is straighter, or even bat wing, or a less exaggerated butterfly shape. Some of the butterfly cuts are far too extreme so we at IBTS suggest our members consider going more toward the bat wing design with either square or diamond cut tails.

The vertical height at the tails and loops on either wing still follow the eye socket rule but can be somewhat finessed, styled, or adjusted to look lower or higher by "scrunching" or "splaying" the wing and loop to look just right. Splay and scrunch styling, or finishing, will be explained in detail in chapter nine.

And remember, it's a pretty safe assumption Adam had absolutely no need for *any* kind of neckwear, much less a tasteful collection of fine quality, handmade bow ties, which would be available online several thousand years later. (That would be today.)

Of course now there are scores of manufacturers and retailers, foreign and domestic, serving thousands of gentlemen buying bow ties purchased over the Internet.

Speaking of buying online...many of our members are painfully aware from their experience that the perceived value, look, size, and quality of the bow ties displayed on their computer's screen too often are not what is promised or delivered. Much to our chagrin, we tear open the much-anticipated package and are forced to suffer or settle for bow ties that don't match our expectations when we bravely exposed our credit card numbers to cyberspace.

Many times bow ties look terrific online but, in real life are difficult to properly tie because of the material, shape, or the lining that just doesn't jell.

However, *sizing* is one of our members' pet peeves. The industry promotes fashion changes to increase sales, but a man's facial features don't change and many a product pictures fail to give dimensions; thus the tie delivered may be too tall at its widest point.

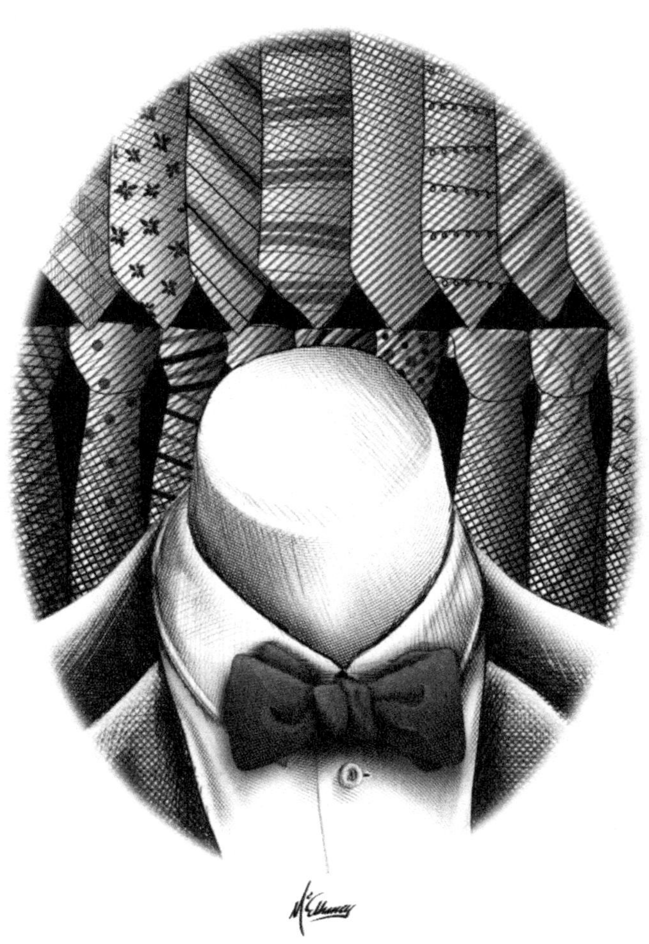

"Wearing a bow tie makes a statement. Almost an act of defiance."

—Rick Kaplan

Chapter Four

Quality vs. Price vs. Value

Most have learned the hard way that cheap prices most often equate to cheap products we will never feel good using. Buying cheap bow ties is risky. A good deal often proves to be inexpensive initially but we warn that wearing a sub-quality bow tie is a mistake we can prevent. And we admit we have learned much vicariously—don't display bow tie foibles around your neck for the world to see! Of course, learning from others' mistakes saves time and embarrassment and helps maintain a healthy self-image!

Even though this is a pseudo Bible, we don't want to preach; however, high price can fool us just as much as off price. Watch out for expensively priced bow ties as well, for they too often miss the mark because of size, shape, look, or material—even more so if they are higher priced because of a designer label.

One of the reasons we are IBTS members is to gain a better understanding of good versus bad as it applies to how, why, and where to find the best handmade quality and value at the best prices. We have done a great deal of research to gain your trust. We hope to earn your respect as a trusted resource. And please believe us when we say learning from like-minded groups or individuals you saves time, money, and embarrassment.

Finding the right price and value is tricky but when you get your arms around all you learn from the Bow Tie Bible the next step is to find the best places on the Internet and in the stores to find that balance between quality, utility, and price to suit your personal long time needs. When we say, "long time needs" we truly mean it because good bow ties last a very long time. The worst thing you can do is compromise so you have to suffer or settle for something is not right for you.

The fact that you are reading this book proves to us you are on the right track!

Chapter Five

Finding bow tie products

Returning to the story... God observed Adam frolicking about with the animals giving them pet names and such. Being omniscient, God quickly realized Adam was much more than just a little bit lonesome. There was no beer, no drinking buddies, and nothing on TV. God could see Adam needed extracurricular activities and maybe even a honey-do list. Put simply, Adam needed a woman!

God foresaw that bow ties would never have a prayer (pun intended) without the help of women around to help tie them. We think this is one of the reasons God gave woman greater manual dexterity and smaller hands. Of course, I am not saying women are not totally superior. It's no secret today women most assuredly control most of the power and wealth on God's earth!

Nevertheless, in many ways Adam had it easier in the Garden of Eden. Today, men are much more confused about women!

Unlike Adam, are challenged to choose between practical, economical, sanitary, and stylish bow ties rather than those "Johnny-come-lately" inventions known as fore-in-hand ties or long ties worn by the masses.

Another reason the Bow Tie Bible had to be written was to help men throughout the world fully understand the bow tie culture and gain insight into better ways to acquire, tie, and wear bow ties to maximize their appeal.

We encourage everyone to visit www.internationalbowtiesociety.com on a somewhat regular basis to follow our “Bow-Blogs” and choose from the various levels of membership along with bow tie tips, products, and services to be found there at discounted prices exclusively to our membership.

Chapter Six

Advent of Clothing and Fashion

Before the fall, Adam and Eve had no concerns about the totally nude thing. And, like we said, Adam didn't have to worry about what kind of tie was best. Words like "style" weren't even in the current vocabulary. Of course, we have no idea what was in his vocabulary. He wasn't known as much of a man of letters since, at that time, there were no letters.

There Adam and Eve were...just the two of them, so impressing Eve wasn't a high priority for Adam. Like the late, great Danny Thomas once quipped, "One day while in the Garden of Eden, Eve asked Adam, 'Do you love me?' Adam, with a confused look, replied, 'Who else?'"

Let's not get diverted. How did fashion really get its start? Glad you asked. Satan came along and observed his "mark" and losing no time convinced the naïve, unsuspecting Eve to sample the forbidden fruit from the tree of knowledge of good and evil. Since misery loves company, after Eve took a bite out of the apple, she seduced unwitting Adam into likewise tasting the delicious forbidden fruit-of-the-day. We might say Adam folded like a cheap suit long before cheap suits came into being!

After dining on the delicious, forbidden fruits, Adam and Eve were banished forever from the Garden of Eden. The story says they were naked and immediately realized they needed to go shopping for clothes! So with that one slipup everything changed and now you know the answer as to how the fashion industry was born. It was truly "a day that will live in infamy" (FDR out of context). Malls were built and traffic became hell on earth!

Eve, bless her sweet heart, was heard using one of the world's oldest excuses. A justification that has stood the test of time longer than any other, "The devil made me do it." And the fashion world has been owing the devil his due to this very day. Now we understand why the devil wears Prada...he gets it wholesale as a quid-pro-quo for what he did for the clothing industry!

Chapter Seven

The Mother of Invention

Necessity, followed by aesthetics, dictates fashion trends. Necessity is the mother of invention.
Aesthetics describes the flamboyant, exuberant aunt that everyone loves!

In the region of the world known as the Holy Lands—the cradle of civilization—there were only two seasons...*hot and hotter*.

Monarchs ruled the world. The *haves* had everything and the *have-nots* had whatever was left over...which was usually zilch. There were three classes of people: the Egyptian ruling class (royalty), the military, and the Hebrew slaves doing what slaves do...slave labor.

The kings and queens wore fabulous jewels around their necks...aesthetically pleasing and necessary for showing off one's wealth and position. At the other end of the social spectrum, the only neckwear slaves needed was whatever leather or steel collars the slave drivers deemed necessary to keep them in line to take care of the royal family and, of course, build the great pyramids and sphinxes.

So, once again you may be wondering what all this has to do with the advent of bow ties? Like I said, necessity is the mother of invention and there was no need for bow ties since there was no practical need to hold collared shirt necks together. The collared shirt hadn't been invented yet. That would come along centuries later in Western Europe... primarily, Paris and London.

"To be one's self, and unafraid whether right or wrong, is more admirable than the easy cowardice of surrender to conformity."

—Irving Wallace

The advent of collared dress shirts

As we mentioned back in Genesis, necks were included as standard equipment, but it wasn't until shirts with structured collars emerged that neckwear would become popular out of necessity.

Collared dress shirts didn't come along until the mid-1700s. The button took longer to be perfected so there was a very practical need for something to hold the collar neat and closed to protect against the chill. Unlike the Middle East; London and Paris were often cold and wet.

Aesthetics were important because of the collar's close proximity to a one's face. Please make a special mental note of this, because the relationship between the size and shape of a properly tied bow tie to one's facial features is the fundamental difference in looking confident versus clownish and trivial when wearing a bow tie.

The world was becoming more fashion conscious and the middle- to upper-middle-class men became increasingly competitive both in their professions and certainly when it comes to impressing women.

Men started fastening their collars together with a narrow strip of cloth. This cloth was the centerpiece or focal point of their fashion image, so they added vivid colors and designs on more precious and expensive cloth to differentiate themselves from their peers as well as complement their wardrobe.

The cloth tied around a gentleman's neck had to be easily tied in the morning and untied each evening, so the next necessity was finding an appropriate knot that would not slip but stay consistently comfortable around one's neck and, at the same time, be aesthetically pleasing, flattering, fashionable, and easily untied. **Thus the bow tie was born!**

Now, today, in a predominately no-tie or long tie world, wearing a bow tie is a statement of nonconformity. Wearing a bow tie properly and confidently is a mark of strong individuality and comfort in one's own skin!

"Every man who is truly a man must learn to be alone in the midst of all the others, and if need be <u>against</u> all others."

—Romain Rolland

HOW TO TIE A BOW TIE:

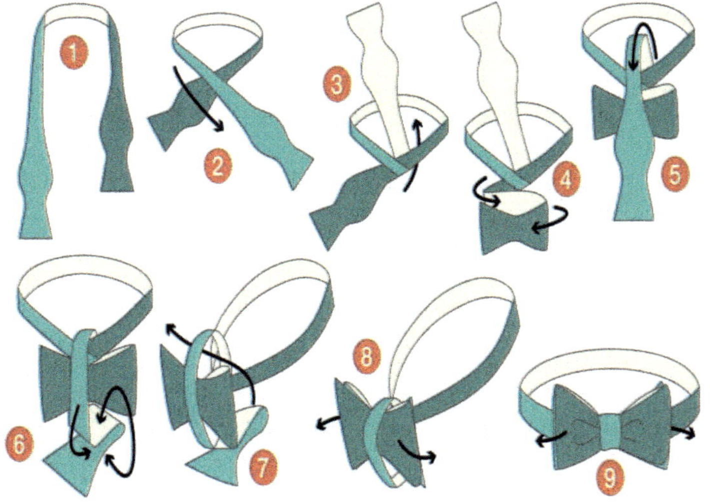

Chapter Eight

It's All about the Knot

Ask any Boy Scout...different knots have specific purposes. Some knots are for holding while others are for slipping. And most knots used in the fashion world are meant to be easily untied. The bow tie is for maintaining a consistent tension around the neck. The neck is not stationary appendage but it needed a knot that wouldn't slip. This is a pivotal point when comparing bow ties to long ties because slipknots tied around anything unstable is guaranteed to fulfill its purpose...to slip!

The bow tie knot was a precursor even to the knot used to tie shoes. The genius behind a bow holding consistent tension on a basic overhand knot became popular because it was not only practical and comfortable but also aesthetically pleasing—if tied and worn properly, no taller or wider than one's eye sockets as a rule of thumb.

"If you stand up and be counted, from time to time you may get yourself knocked down. But remember this: A man flattened by an opponent can get up again. A man flattened by conformity stays down for good."

—Thomas J. Watson

Think about something most men almost never consider. When we tie our shoes we put whatever tension we desire on the initial overhand knot to start. The bow you then craft has a useful purpose in that it maintains the desired tautness for comfort with no perceptible slippage all day long.

Using a slipknot on any moving part of the body makes no sense. You would be tightening and/or loosening it numerous times all day just exactly as men do with long ties! Presumably, the only time anyone needs to retie one's shoes is when laces become untied accidentally or intentionally. The properly tied bow tie only becomes untied on purpose. Many bow tie wearers go for the George Clooney look by untying the bow tie and casually allowing tails to drape demonstrating it is not pre-tied or clip-on.

Expensive silk long ties affixed with slipknots (like inverted hangman's nooses) were originally designed to cover and protect dress shirts. As these, dare we say, "bibs" began to be made with high-priced silks they lost their purpose but remained in vogue for aesthetics despite their lack of practicality.

Long ties continue to become more expensive, plus they are uncomfortable due to the fact that slipknots inevitably slip loose with the movement of the neck numerous times each day. As we said, slipknots used with long ties are designed to *slip*, and thus require constant and continual tightening and loosening.

Each time a man tightens a long tie he typically overcompensates, thinking that tighter equals more time between retightening. This curious game defies common sense because he made it uncomfortable for the sake of convenience and, minutes later, loosens it with his fingers for comfort. This goes on while he complains it's too tight or too loose! Is there anyone reading this that doesn't see the irony?

We choose not to accept ever again the excuse "I never learned to tie a bow tie," allowing men to safely fall back on long ties without seriously considering the pros and cons of bucking conformity.

We believe tying a bow tie is easier than tying a long tie after one learns. Many a twelve-year-old has mastered the feat with little help.

Plus, if a man is convinced he will try wearing a bow tie he will find a way to tie it. There are scores of YouTube videos showing everyone from seven-year-olds to Playboy bunnies giving detailed instruction on how to tie one. Unfortunately, there is little or no mention of how or why to wear bow ties so, with the help of Adam, Eve, Moses, and David we will relish the idea of moving forward doing God's work!

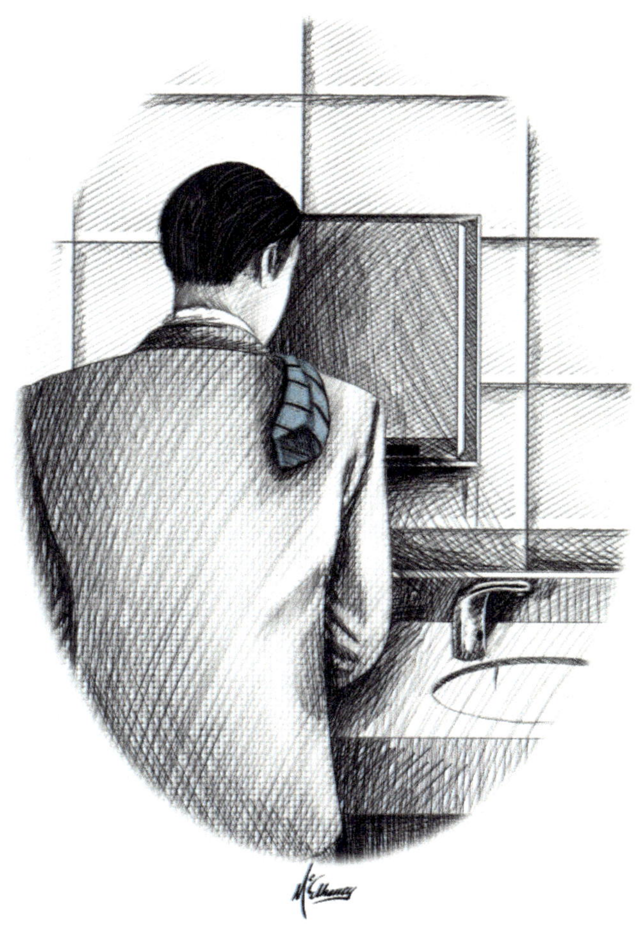

Wash hands once - touch germ-infested tie twice?

Chapter Nine

Styling with Scrunch and Splay

Once you master the tying of the bow tie, there is one more subtle but critical step many YouTube demos call styling, or finishing. This is the process of achieving a look that is stylish and proper but not to the point that it is so neat that it seems pre-tied. You want a happy medium between dressy-but-casual but definitely not pre-tied.

The following explanation will be, at best, confusing, so in making it more understandable we must define the parts of the standard bow tie.

Picture this in your mind's eye. A bow is the convergence of two loops and two tails with a knot in the middle. Each side, or wing, of the bow has one tail and one loop. On one wing the loop is in front and the tail is in back; on the other wing the tail is in front and the loop is in back. Are you following?

Understand that the term "pulling outward" means pulling straight toward your shoulders. "Folding forward" means taking the entire wing on either or both sides to pull forward to create a fold crease adjacent to either side right at the knot.

"Pinching" requires both hands and means taking the wings between your fingers and bending them forward horizontally while holding them out to the sides. This creates a horizontal crease on the wing.

It is important that you distinguish the difference between folding forward and pinching forward. We suggest rereading prior to trying the "splay" and "scrunch" step or you will lose focus and possibly become discouraged.

To tighten the knot, first make both wings of the bow symmetrical, but not totally even, but as even as you wish. Alternatively, pull the tails and loops on both sides then pull both loops at the same time to tighten. Pulling the tails *unties* everything! (Darn...start over!)

The next step is called "scrunching" and it is just as it sounds. You take both wings of both sides of your tied and tightened bow tie simultaneously with your thumbs, pointers, and middle fingers pinching both ends of the wings forward while also pushing both wings horizontally toward the knot thus making the bow both shorter and narrower.

Scrunching is not only handy in making the bow tie look less flat and pre-tied but also, if you twist it forward without splaying, it can take a ¼ inch off the height of a bow tie that may be a bit too tall to start with.

"The supreme lesson of any education should be to think for yourself and to be yourself; absent this attainment, education creates dangerous, stupefying conformity."

—Bryant H. McGill

"Splaying" is almost the opposite of scrunching—but not quite. To splay, you scrunch first then scrunch in reverse. But, instead of twisting forward to make the bow tie wings look shorter you hold your thumb and pointer with the loop and the tip between them on both sides together moving each in opposing directions to create a ¼-inch to ½-inch *taller* look.
(Hint: When you play cards you "splay" them in your hand to see them all at the same time.)

Whereas these steps are important to getting the vertical or height you need, believe us when we say it is easier to make a slightly too small bow tie look taller than a too tall one to look shorter. Of course if all bow ties were "bat wing" style at 1 ¾ - 2 inch height it wouldn't take much styling at all to flatter the facial and neck structure of most men on God's green earth!

Remember, dressy-yet-casual but definitely self-tied and not so neat or straight as to appear pre-tied.

“ You can’t dribble on bow ties.”
—Dr. Seuss

Chapter Ten

Protecting ties with shirts?

From time to time one may have found oneself or another unbuttoning a few front shirt buttons to stuff a long tie inside. This bizarre activity, along with flipping the tie over the shoulder with the good intention of protecting it from foreign matter that might spread disease or ruin the tie is commonplace.

Maybe this is the reason tie bars have all but disappeared from the men's fashion scene. They hold the long tie in harm's way—right under the holes-in-one's-head and where three meals a day are transported from the plate to the mouth.

The irony of these safeguarding activities is twofold:

First: The initial purpose of the draped long tie has been reversed from the protector of the shirt to being protected by the shirt. It, de facto, lost its job, its purpose, its practicality, and therefore, its necessity!

Second: Every time one's fingers touch the silk tie—ostensibly to protect it from food, spittle, or mucus—microorganisms are transferred to or from that tie to grow and spread as a result of that careless or unnoticed accident during lunch! Fact is, the majority of harmful bacteria come not from the elements to which it's exposed but from the wearers' own hands!

What we are pointing out—ad nauseam—is long ties remain aesthetically pleasing and socially conforming even though it is festering with unseen harmful bacteria it collects as the unwitting wearer futilely tries to protect its look all day long by simply touching it with his hands. This is especially true in the men's room when a man grabs his far less than germ-free silk tie with his bacteria-laden fingertips to toss over his shoulder both before and after using the toilet, the urinal, and (drum roll please) before and after hand washings!

Then why don't we launder, dry clean, or otherwise sanitize the long tie every day? Only God and anyone whose tried it before knows.

It begs the rhetorical question, "Is it impossible, impractical, or both to clean and sanitize a long tie?"
By now you know the answer...Wear a good bow tie. You properly tie it in the morning with washed hands; it never gets in the way, and with little more than one tug, preferably with a clean hand, you untie it when you're ready.

Chapter Eleven

Bow Ties? Long Ties?

Let's summarize...

Comfort Factor...

Why are we going through such a lengthy description of how a bow maintains its stability and tension of an overhand knot? Because through some misguided reasoning the fashion industry succeeded in selling to the general public the idea that the long tie is a practical method of protecting the front of a shirt. They then preceded in further convincing gentlemen to instruct their children to tie them with slipknots that, as I previously described in detail, have to be retightened and then loosened continually all during the day! Again...slipknots are designed to slip. They are *not* designed to hold or maintain a desired, and comfortable, amount of tension. We ask again...would you tie your shoes with a slipknot?

Anyone who has ever worn a standard fore-in-hand tie perhaps heard himself complaining to anyone in earshot of its discomfort. The fact is, long ties get in the way. The reason men are so willingly vociferous about this is that everyone around them shares the same complaint!

Long ties are unsanitary...

There was an article in the *Wall Street Journal* a couple years back about long ties being a health hazard. A growing number of hospitals are disallowing doctors from wearing them for that reason.

Why would the fashion industry continue to promote a silk bib doing what it was intended to do that can't be tossed in the laundry daily for cleanliness and protection against harmful bacteria?

We said it earlier, but consider this...a good silk long tie can cost as much or more than a nice cotton dress shirt but the silk tie cannot be laundered as can a shirt. It is rare that any man sends his favorite silk tie to the cleaners, for fear it will be ruined. Many dry cleaners will no longer accept that risk as well. Most men can tell you about the first (and last) time they sent one out to the dry cleaner!

As we illustrated previously, the wearer must handle the silk tie incessantly each day to keep it safe, yet doing so only makes it more unsanitary because fingertips are the primary source of germs, oil, and dirt.

And any mother can tell you their children's bibs require washing and sanitizing every day in hot water and soap for good health. Now we see why children's bibs are made of plastic or terry cloth! We have never heard of bibs made of finely printed or woven silk.

And, a word to the wise...don't stick a silk tie in the washer and dryer or put spot remover on silk. Just stop wasting money on long ties!

Quality long ties are expensive...

Long ties can cost 20-30 percent more than bow ties of exactly the same make and material. They must be replaced far more often simply because their original purpose has been compromised. They don't travel well and they wrinkle easily.

Bow ties last four to five times longer and hardly ever have to be replaced because of a Balsamic vinaigrette stain caused by a casually dropped tomato wedge.

Regular bow tie wearers will readily tell us, with some certainty, they can never remember *ever* ruining a bow tie due to stains from foreign matter or from the oil, dirt, or bacteria from constant touching.

Bow ties do not ever need to be discarded due to changes in fashion trends. Bow ties should—if sized correctly—complement one's face and neck size, which remain approximately the same size.

Bow ties are unquestionably a better investment of one's clothing dollars thus allowing larger collections and greater variety of assorted colors and materials—if one makes informed choices.

Long ties are pretty, but also pretty impractical...

Anything in God's creation that is simultaneously *un*comfortable, *un*sanitary, *and* expensive is impractical—by any *definition*. It begs the question, "Why do men today buy and wear long ties instead of bows more than fifty-to-one!"

You can readily see why the fashion industry promotes the long tie trend. They want us all buried in your cleanest one!

Image

Because long ties are the status quo by over fifty-to-one, it makes little or no unique lifestyle statement. It is the norm. It only demonstrates the wearers' conformity. Some of us want and need the contrast a bow tie makes. Some of us prefer to show a little individualism among the entire uniformity!

Bow ties are not just a fashion option in a long tie world. A properly sported bow tie is a personal lifestyle statement of a well dressed and educated, discerning individualist comfortable in his own skin.

Chapter Twelve

Bow Tie Golden Rule

"Do unto others, as you would have them do unto you."
Sound familiar?
The Bow Tie Golden Rule applies to these next short anecdotal comments:

Let's say a friend or acquaintance asks a seemingly harmless question, "Did you tie that bow tie yourself?"

We know that if you're like most bow tie people you feel offended by the suggestion you might be wearing a pre-tied, or worse, a clip-on bow tie.
But before you overreact contemptuously, just take a deep breath and remain smiling and affable. Respond as sociably as possible, saying, "Let me ask you this: Did you tie that tie [or those shoes] yourself?"

Reply with no malice while showing true curiosity and you get your point across about the absurdness of their question without stepping on any toes. People just don't know they have mildly offended a bow tie wearer with that absurd question. One should be flattered that we tied it right so it wouldn't look pre-tied!

When someone compliments us on how our bow tie looks, stating, “I love bow ties. I would wear one if I knew how to tie it like you,” we react immediately yet respectfully without a hint of condescension, saying, “So if I taught you a simple way to tie a bow tie, would you begin wearing them?”

At that point he usually stammers and backpedals or smiles and remains mute. As the conversation progresses he comes to the realization that he might not have been completely forthright in his original statement. He may harbor some other subconscious feelings about stepping out from the norm. The status quo of conformity is just so darn comfortable...

That is how to comply with the spirit of the Golden Rule and effectively get the point over without hurting someone’s feelings or seeming arrogant.

Chapter Thirteen

Ten Commandments Annotated

Most of the big ten are self-explanatory, however some clarification is helpful to achieve a full understanding.

I. *Thou shalt never wear pre-tied or "clip-on" bow ties*. Pre-tied and clip-ons are for kids under age 12 or arthritic elders who have difficulty lifting their arms. It is our nightmare that we see ourselves in the casket and some thoughtless twerp put a pre-tied or clip-on on our lifeless cadaver. That would almost be as bad as a long tie...almost!

II. *Thou shalt not wear bow ties horizontally wider or vertically taller than your eye sockets*. Suffice it to say size *does* matter when it comes to bow ties—so does shape!

A fine quality silk or seasonal natural fiber bow tie with rich colors can make the wearer look like a vaudeville comedian or a circus clown if it's even as little as one-eighth inch larger (taller or wider) than one's eye sockets. One-eighth inch *smaller* is perfectly acceptable.

A great-looking bow tie is much more proper and professional if congruent with one's face, neck, and head size. The fashion industry profits by promoting size-up or size-down trends to create obsolescence to increase sells—but remember, the structure of one's face, neck, and head rarely change after adolescence.

We believe that 95 percent of men have remarkably similar facial features. The most prevalent sizes are 2 to 2¼ tall by 4½ to 4 ¾ inches wide. Most eye sockets measure about 2 inches high from the lower part of the eyebrow to the highest part of the cheekbone. When we measure from temple to temple horizontally, it comes to about 4 1/4 inches. Men with larger heads appear to have smaller faces as a rule. We observe men have bigger and smaller heads, however their eyes and facial measurements do not appear to vary commensurately.

Have you ever noticed how large a very young child's eyes appear when they are toddlers and how much smaller their eyeballs look a few years later?
Eyeballs don't grow perceptibly past late childhood. The face just had to catch up with the eyeballs!

If one has a 15½-inch neck, they may have to set the sizing gauge (some bow ties have them; some don't) to about 14½ inches so as not to exceed the overall horizontal measurement that does not wing-out horizontally beyond your eye sockets or the width of your neck—whichever is more narrow.

Many of our members buy bow ties that are 1 3/4 to 2 inches tall at their tallest point. It is better to buy a bow tie a little smaller rather than too large. It's easier to "splay" to increase the height than to "scrunch" to reduce the height to fit with your facial features. It also make a less "pre-tied-too-neat" appearance.

To achieve an approximate 2–2¼-inch height that's complementary to most men's faces, splay (spread) the ends of the bow tie after it is tied with the forefingers and thumbs. If you happen to be wearing the standard Brooks Brothers bow tie you may have to scrunch the ends to achieve the desired 2-inch height. On a 2-inch tie you may both scrunch and splay to achieve the most natural finished look and further avoid that pre-tied, too neat appearance mentioned earlier.

By properly tying a free-style, quality, handmade bow tie and mastering this scrunch and/or splay finishing exercise, one gets a consistent look that adequately complies with numerals I, II, and III of the Bow Tie Ten Commandments.

III. *Thou shalt not wear bow ties so neat and symmetrical as to appear pre-tied.* This was adequately covered and explained in the first two commandments. Remember, you never want it to appear too neat, because the bow tie looks best if it demonstrates a little personality, or *je ne sais quoi.*

IV. *Thou shalt not wait past age 12 to learn how to properly tie a bow tie.* Learn to tie a bow tie by age 12. Don't "wish you had" when you can be "glad you did." It is not that hard to learn once you decide you really want to learn!

V. *Thou shalt volunteer to help others learn to properly tie bow ties.* It's the basic idea behind the Golden Rule.

VI. *Thou shalt assist others in understanding how and why one would choose to wear bow ties, especially if they are relatives.* Education is so much more fulfilling when we know how things work best and why they are important.

VII. *Thou shalt tactfully correct others wearing bow ties improperly.* Don't let others' lack of education hurt the bow tie cause, the culture, or the renaissance. Talk with them tactfully with your heart in the right place and they will thank you for it now and/or later.

VIII. *Thou shalt learn how to communicate to others why you prefer bow ties as a positive alternative to long ties.* If you're reading this, you are well on your way there. You'll build confidence by just doing it consistently!

IX. *Thou shalt own at least two dozen properly sized and shaped quality, handmade bow ties that you love to wear.* This one is also self-explanatory. Your membership in IBTS will help. We vet each resource and then negotiate better pricing exclusively for our membership so we get better pricing and value on first run as well as clearance goods.

X. *Thou shalt suggest friends, family, and colleagues to go to International Bow Tie Society and join free or pay a little for more benefits today even if they are not into bow ties.* The more members we have, the better the benefits for all. Membership is still free. (Of course you can buy a premium membership and get much more value.) Tell everyone you know and everyone you meet to go to www.InternationalBowTieSociety.com.

Chapter Fourteen

The 23rd Psalm- Bow Tie Version

The Lord is my shepherd I shall not want.

He blesses my father's heart.
My dad taught me to tie long ties like his dad and his dad's father before him,
But this conflicted my soul:
My dad unknowingly led me down the paths of conformity for he just knew no other way.

Yea, though I walk through the room with my stylish bow tie,
I will fear no dissension.
Discerning individualism and confidence—they comfort me.

Thou prepares table before me in the presence of the long tie conformists.
Thou anointed my salad plate with oils;
The salad dressing runneth over.
Expensive long ties met their fate from wayward splatters.
Surely goodness and mercy shall follow me
All the days of my life;
For my bow tie escaped harm will dwell ever clean and fresh in the house of the Lord,
Or wherever I may go. Forever.

Chapter Fifteen

The Heredity Conundrum

Dads throughout history unknowingly brainwashed their sons (too strong a word?). Correction: Dads have lovingly suggested, with no malice and no mention of other alternatives, that their sons wear long ties when the occasion calls for wearing neckwear.

Long ties have been the status quo for scores of years. There has been no thought or discussion of bow ties as a positive, or negative, alternative to these more expensive, less comfortable, impractical, unsanitary silk bibs. Fathers and grandfathers have innocently influenced their sons in their youth when they were most naïve and vulnerable to conform to the norm.

Part of the irony is that the average dad rarely spoke favorably about *any* type of neckwear and never broached the subject of why neckwear of any sort had practical, useful, or positive purposes. Parents persuaded their young charges verbally and nonverbally that wearing ties was a necessary evil...a curse always to be eschewed!

In other words, when a young man has an occasion requiring neckwear, he is either ignorant, uninformed, or misinformed of his options and, of course, isn't in any way motivated to consider self-tied bow ties versus long ties. It's not his fault, it's not his father's fault, or his grandfather's fault...it's heredity's fault!

Social peer pressure and parental influence are, to a great extent, responsible for what we consider anti–bow tie prejudice that is passed down through generations and influencing conventional social etiquette. Then again, as previously noted, anti-*any*-neckwear bias is in the same boat!

Chapter Sixteen

Revelation to Resurgence

Naturally, when one reads or hears the word "tie" or "necktie" nowadays we immediately think of the long tie. It's a tie and that other is a "bow tie." Why? Bow ties were here well before long ties. Not only do they pre-date long ties, they were the focal point of a well-dressed man's sense of style and self-image.
Bow ties have always been less expensive, more comfortable, more sanitary, and longer lasting; thus allowing men to collect a greater assortment to choose from for their wardrobe. Bow ties never get in the way, they pack and travel better, and now, since long ties are the status quo, bow ties make a statement of confidence, style, discernment, and individuality. And if worn correctly, bow ties are more flattering to a gentleman's facial features thus promoting an image of a very well educated, enlightened, and well-dressed man comfortable in his own skin!

The fashion world is aware the long tie has outlived its practical purpose for being necessary to protect a man's dress shirt. Yes, long ties are indeed aesthetically pleasing, and yes most of us were taught to tie one in their youth; however, we believe the negatives outweigh the positives for those now, hopefully enlightened individualists.

In this age of mobile technology one of the negatives associated with the bow tie culture has been virtually eliminated. Now, there are scores of retailers that have picked up on the idea that bow tie people enjoy shopping over the Internet. We at IBTS would like to think we had a little to do with more and more Internet outlets displaying the dimensions and shapes that are congruent with our message and your needs regarding how the size of the bow tie is crucial to the image and self-confidence of the wearer.

Frankly the fashion industry doesn't believe it can afford to believe what has been written here and doesn't want the world to believe in anything that might cost them money in the short run even though it can make them more in the future. They deny the value of change because they need the status to *stay static* until they deem it time to arbitrarily change it!

Replacing long silk ties that cannot efficiently or effectively be washed and sanitized is *big* business for the industry. Couple that with man-made "fashion cycles" of narrow ties today, wide tomorrow, and medium the next and it represents even bigger business at your expense!

Consider that bow ties shouldn't be fashion sensitive when it comes to size changes because properly proportioned, flattering, stylish bow ties will remain the same size if the wearer's eye sockets remain the same size!

Some of our members—I am the worst for this—have a confession to make. We have 1½ to 2 inch bow ties in our collections that are twenty and thirty years old! They still look new; you can't get food on them, we need not touch them but to tie and untie—hopefully with clean hands—so we wear when they fit our attire, the occasion, our attitude, our style, and our mood. And we feel as good in them now as any we bought last week or last month.

"That's how we've always done it" is the primary reason most men have for not considering bow ties in a long tie world—however that can change with a little education and your help!

We humbly suggest men start by measuring their eye sockets and the width of their necks and go online or in person to retail stores or manufacturers and buy a freestyle black tie that is narrow enough to complement his facial features. You may find 1½ to 2¼ inch height is hard to find but it is definitely worth the hunt. If "getting it right" is not one's goal, then what is?

But please be cautious. Many excellent clothiers and manufacturers have never had much motivation to research, study, or understand bow ties. They believe the customer is always right, however it is *their* responsibility to insure the customer has the best information so they won't make mistakes.

Conclusion

Bow ties are coming back—but not for long if men throughout the world don't get it right and understand how and why to wear them.

A bow tie resurgence can grow if every well-dressed thinking person reads and appreciates the message conveyed by the International Bow Tie Society website and especially the Bow Tie Bible.

This is the first ever Bow Tie Bible, so it is suitable that we again seek your absolution for the implication that every man should wear bow ties. If bow ties were the norm, then there would be no need for a statement of discerning individuality. The status quo is the status quo. If every man in the room were wearing properly tied and sized quality bow ties there would be no need for this book.

Discerning individualists need to make a statement. It is in their DNA. And for that statement to be heard and have meaning they must stand out from the conforming crowd.

If Adam and Eve had not disobeyed God in the first place the world would be an altogether different place. We are imperfect people living a short time in an imperfect world. It has been said that we are the sum total of the people we meet and the books we read. We would add—and the bow ties that we wear!

Postlude

Congratulations to you on reading the Bow Tie Bible. If you liked it let us know at: Internationalbowtiesociety@gmail.com, and if you don't mind, share it with other like-minded discerning individualists. And if you haven't already, go to www.InternationalBowTieSociety.com. And join!

If you liked the Bow Tie Bible and believe its message should be heard, would you kindly consider telling all your friends, your e-mail buddies, and your social media followers about us? Maybe you could suggest they go to www.InternationalBowTieSociety.com and join, even if they are not into bow ties so they can have some fun while better understanding and appreciating the bow tie culture and what it's like to sport a bow tie in a long tie world! If you use Facebook check out: Facebook.com/internationalbowtiesociety

And finally, please don't miss the opportunity to get a case of Bow Tie Bibles for gifts for any occasion! They make unique host and hostess gifts. We hope you can and will use your imagination to spread the word and have some fun at the same time. Your friends will appreciate it and, if you wear bow ties, you will appreciate their understanding why you do and maybe, just maybe, they will wonder why anyone ever wore long ties in the first place!

CPSIA information can be obtained
at www.ICGtesting.com
Printed in the USA
LVOW06*1312091216
516577LV00005B/9/P

9 780692 606926